The People's President and India's Missile Man

Dr. A.P.J. Abdul Kalam

Introduction:

Dr. A.P.J. Abdul Kalam, fondly called the "People's President" and "India's Rocket Man," was a visionary leader, a scientist and statesman who left an indelible mark on India and the world. His life and achievements continue to inspire people around the world. In this ebook, we will trace the incredible journey of Dr. A.P.J. Abdul Kalam from his humble beginnings to becoming one of India's most revered and beloved leaders.

Birth of the Legend :

Dr. A.P.J. Abdul Kalam was born on October 15, 1931, in Rameswaram, a small island town in the southern state of Tamil Nadu, India. He was born into a humble household and his parents, Jainulabdeen and Ashiamma, instilled strong family values and a sense of simplicity in him from an early age. Rameswaram, with its rich cultural heritage and spiritual significance, had a profound impact on Dr. Kalam's character and upbringing, shaping his worldview and laying the foundation for his remarkable journey as a scientist, leader, and visionary.

Early Life:

Despite financial difficulties, Kalam's family instilled in him at a young age the values of hard work, perseverance, and the importance of education.

As a child, Kalam was naturally curious and inquisitive. He was fascinated by the world around him and often made experiments and observations. He had a keen interest in maths, science, and technology and spent hours reading books and exploring scientific concepts. Kalam's curiosity and thirst for knowledge were encouraged by his family and teachers, who encouraged his academic pursuits and instilled in him a love of learning.

In his early life, Kalam's education played a crucial role in shaping his character and career. His thirst for knowledge, curiosity, and determination to excel despite challenges were critical to his academic achievements and later success as a renowned scholar and leader. Kalam's early life experiences also instilled in him a deep sense of humility, compassion, and a strong work ethic that stayed with him throughout his life.

In summary, Dr. A.P.J. Abdul Kalam's early life was marked by humble beginnings, resilience, and a passion for learning. Despite financial difficulties, he prioritized his education and pursued his academic interests with determination and perseverance. Kalam's early education laid the foundation for his remarkable career as a scholar, leader, and visionary. His story continues to inspire generations of people to follow their passions, overcome obstacles, and strive for excellence in their pursuit.

Education:

The education of Dr. A.P.J. Abdul Kalam , played a crucial role in shaping his life and career. Despite numerous challenges and obstacles, Dr. Kalam's relentless pursuit of knowledge, lifelong learning, and commitment to academic excellence made him one of the most renowned scholars and leaders in India's history.

Dr. Kalam's early education was marked by humble beginnings. He was born in a small village called Rameswaram in Tamil Nadu, India, and his family had limited financial resources. However, his parents, Jainulabdeen and Ashiamma, instilled in him from an early age a deep appreciation for education and a love of learning. Dr. Kalam's father was an imam at a local mosque and a boat owner, and his mother was a housewife. Despite their modest means, they ensured that he received a good education.

Dr. Kalam's formal education began at Schwartz High School in Ramanathapuram, Tamil Nadu. He was a bright student who showed a keen interest in science and mathematics. He excelled in his studies and received several scholarships that helped him continue his education. However, the death of his father when he was just 15 years old forced him to take up odd jobs to support his family while he continued his studies.

In 1950, Dr. Kalam enrolled at St. Joseph's College in Tiruchirapalli to study physics. He graduated with a bachelor's degree in physics and then went on to study aeronautical engineering at the Madras Institute of Technology (MIT) in 1954. At MIT, Dr. Kalam's passion for engineering and technology was awakened, and he began to dream of a career in aerospace engineering.

Dr. Kalam's thirst for knowledge and determination to pursue higher education led him to pursue a master's degree in aerospace engineering at the Indian Institute of Science (IISc) in Bangalore. However, due to financial constraints, he was unable to complete the program and had to return to Rameswaram.

Despite this setback, Dr. Kalam was not deterred in his passion for learning. He expanded his knowledge through self-study and voracious reading. He spent hours in the library devouring books on science, technology, and aviation. He also actively participated in technical forums and debated with other scientists and engineers, demonstrating his keen intellect and thirst for knowledge.

Dr. Kalam's relentless pursuit of knowledge and exceptional abilities caught the attention of the Indian scientific community, and he was offered a position with the Defense Research and Development Organization (DRDO) in 1958. This marked the beginning of his illustrious career as a scientist and set him on the path of remarkable achievements in the field of science and technology.

Throughout his career, Dr. Kalam placed great emphasis on education and self-improvement. He continued his education, completed advanced courses in defense management and technology, and received numerous honorary doctorates from prestigious institutions around the world. He also served as a visiting professor at various universities, sharing his knowledge and experience with students and researchers.

Dr. Kalam's belief in the power of education as a catalyst for personal and social growth was unwavering. He often emphasized the need to prioritize education and skill development, especially among youth, and advocated for the creation of a knowledge-based society. He believed that education was the key to realizing the full potential of individuals and communities, and he worked tirelessly to promote science and technology education throughout India.

In summary, Dr. A.P.J. Abdul Kalam's education played an important role in shaping his life and career. His thirst for knowledge, his dedication to education helped him to shape his career in Rocket Science.

Remarkable Career :

Dr. A.P.J. Abdul Kalam's distinguished career with the Indian Space Research Organization (ISRO) and the Defense Research and Development Organization (DRDO) is a testament to his exceptional scientific acumen, leadership skills, and unwavering commitment to advancing India's defense and space capabilities. Kalam's contributions to these prestigious organizations have left an indelible mark on India's scientific and technological landscape, earning him the title "Missile Man of India"

After joining DRDO as a senior scientific assistant in 1958, Kalam's career quickly took off. He worked on a variety of projects, including developing indigenous guided missiles and researching radar systems. Kalam's expertise in missile technology led him to become project director of India's first indigenous satellite launcher (SLV-III) in the 1970s, successfully launching India's first satellite, Rohini, into orbit in 1980. This historic achievement made India a space nation and laid the foundation for the development of India's space program.

Kalam's illustrious career with ISRO began in the 1960s when he joined the organization as director of the Satellite Launch Vehicle (SLV) project. He played a critical role in the development of India's space program and was instrumental in the successful development and launch of several satellite missions, including the Polar Satellite Launch Vehicle (PSLV) and the Geosynchronous Satellite Launch Vehicle (GSLV). Under his leadership, ISRO achieved several milestones, including the successful launch of India's first lunar mission, Chandrayaan-1, in 2008.

Apart from his contributions to space exploration, Kalam's career at DRDO was equally impressive. He played a critical role in the development of Indian missile technology and led the Integrated Guided Missile Development Program (IGMDP) in the 1980s and 1990s. Kalam was instrumental in the successful development of India's Agni series of ballistic missiles, Prithvi surface-to-surface missiles, and Akash surface-to-air missiles, among others. His vision, technical expertise, and leadership were instrumental in establishing India's capabilities in missile technology and strengthening its defense capabilities.

One of Kalam's most significant achievements at DRDO was the successful test firing of the Pokhran- II nuclear-capable ballistic missile in 1998, a test that catapulted India into the league of nuclear-armed nations and strengthened its strategic deterrence capabilities. Kalam's leadership and contributions to India's missile and defense programs earned him national and international recognition as a leading scientist and technocrat.

Kalam's career at ISRO and DRDO consisted not only of technical achievements, but also of leadership and mentorship. He was known for his inspirational leadership style that emphasized teamwork, innovation, and integration. He motivated and mentored countless young scientists and engineers, instilling in them a passion for science, technology and nation building. Kalam's leadership style was distinguished by his humility, integrity, and unwavering commitment to serving the nation.

People's President :

Dr. A.P.J. Abdul Kalam's presidency in India from 2002 to 2007 was marked by his visionary leadership, commitment to youth empowerment, and unwavering dedication to national development. Affectionately called "the people's president," Kalam left an indelible mark during his tenure in the country's highest office and continues to inspire generations of Indians.

As India's 11th president, Kalam brought a fresh and innovative approach to the role of president. He was known for his down-to-earth demeanor, humility and accessibility to the common people. Kalam's presidency was distinguished by his strong focus on science, technology, education and youth empowerment, which he saw as important drivers of India's progress and development.

One of Kalam's notable contributions during his presidency was his emphasis on harnessing technology for national development. He envisioned India as a technologically advanced nation and advocated the use of science and technology in various fields, including agriculture, health care, and education. Kalam's vision of a developed and technologically empowered India earned him the nickname "President of the People" as he sought to connect with the masses and inspire them to scientific temperament and innovation.

Kalam was also a strong advocate of education and youth empowerment. He believed that India's youth were the country's greatest asset and needed to be nurtured to reach their full potential. He extensively visited educational institutions across the country, conversing with students and inspiring them to dream big and work towards their goals. Kalam's interactions with the youth were marked by his motivational speeches urging them to be proactive, innovative and committed to nation building.

During his presidency, Kalam also worked to promote inclusivity and social harmony. He advocated the importance of unity in diversity and stressed the need to promote tolerance, mutual respect and understanding among different communities and religions. Kalam's efforts to promote communal harmony and social cohesion earned him widespread respect and admiration.

In addition to his vision and initiatives, Kalam's presidency was also marked by his exemplary behavior and integrity. He was known for his simplicity, humility and incorruptibility, and led by example. Kalam was known as a president who connected with people, listened to their concerns, and inspired them with his words and actions.

Kalam's tenure as President of India was not without challenges. He was criticized for some of his decisions and actions, and there were debates over certain issues during his presidency. But Kalam's unwavering commitment to the well-being of the nation, his visionary leadership, and his exceptional personal qualities endeared him to people from all walks of life.

Even after his term as president ended, Kalam continued to inspire and influence India's youth through his lectures, writings and public appearances. He remained a highly respected figure in India and around the world until his death in 2015.

In summary, Dr. A.P.J. Abdul Kalam's presidency in India was marked by his visionary leadership, commitment to youth empowerment, and unwavering dedication to national development. He left an indelible mark on the country's social, economic, and technological landscape, and his legacy continues to inspire generations of Indians. Kalam, who is fondly referred to as "the people's president," will always be remembered as a true visionary, patriot and leader who embodied integrity, humility and dedication in the service of the nation.

Personal Life and Legacy :

Kalam's personal life was also marked by his deep-rooted patriotism and unwavering love for his country, India. He was deeply committed to the welfare of his fellow citizens and dedicated his life to the progress and development of the nation. He believed that the youth of India are the torchbearers of change and worked tirelessly to help them realize their full potential.

Kalam's personal life was also marked by his unwavering integrity, humility and simplicity. He led a frugal and disciplined lifestyle, always putting the needs of others before his own. Despite his many achievements and awards, he remained down-to-earth and always valued the contributions and ideas of others. Kalam was known for his warm and approachable nature, always willing to listen and engage with people from all walks of life.

Kalam's legacy is one that inspires people around the world. His contributions to science, technology and national development are unparalleled. A renowned scientist, he played a critical role in the development of India's missile and space programs, which made the country self-sufficient in key defense technologies. Kalam's work in the Indian Space Research Organization (ISRO) and the Defense Research and Development Organization (DRDO) earned him numerous awards and honors, including the prestigious Bharat Ratna, India's highest civilian award.

Kalam's legacy, however, extends beyond his achievements as a scientist and leader. He was a great teacher and mentor, always willing to share his knowledge and wisdom with the younger generation. He inspired millions of students with his lectures, speeches, and writings, challenging them to dream big, work hard, and contribute to the nation's progress. Kalam's inspirational leadership style of vision, integrity, and ability to connect with people continues to be a role model for leaders and individuals alike.

Kalam's legacy also includes his unwavering commitment to social causes such as education, health care and rural development. He passionately advocated for the marginalized in society and worked tirelessly for their welfare. He believed in the power of education to change lives and worked tirelessly for literacy and education of underprivileged communities, especially in rural areas.

Awards :

Dr. A.P.J. Abdul Kalam has received numerous awards and recognitions for his outstanding contributions to various fields during his illustrious career as a scientist, leader and visionary. Some of the major awards bestowed upon him are:

Bharat Ratna: In 1997, Dr. Abdul Kalam received the Bharat Ratna, India's highest civilian award, for his exceptional contributions to the field of science and technology and his exemplary leadership in the country's defense and space programs.

Padma Vibhushan: Dr. Kalam was awarded the Padma Vibhushan, India's second highest civilian award, in 1990 for his exceptional contributions to the field of science and technology.

Padma Bhushan: In 1981, Dr. Kalam received the Padma Bhushan, India's third highest civilian award, in recognition of his outstanding contributions to the field of science and technology.

Indira Gandhi Award for National Integration: In 1997, Dr. Kalam was honored with the Indira Gandhi Award for National Integration in recognition of his exemplary efforts in promoting national integration, communal harmony and social cohesion in India.

King Charles II Medal: In 2007, Dr. Kalam was awarded the King Charles II Medal by the Royal Society, United Kingdom, in recognition of his outstanding contributions to science and technology.

Von Braun Award: In 2013, Dr. Kalam was posthumously awarded the Von Braun Award by the National Space Society, USA, in recognition of his significant contributions to the advancement of space science and technology.

Hoover Medal: In 2008, Dr. Kalam was awarded the Hoover Medal by the ASME Foundation, USA, for his outstanding contributions to public service, leadership, and engineering.

Doctorates: Dr. Kalam has received honorary doctorates from over 40 universities around the world, including the College of Wolverhampton, UK; Carnegie Mellon College, USA; Nanyang Technological College, Singapore; and Moscow State College, Russia, in recognition of his exceptional contributions to science, technology, and leadership.

These are just a few of the many awards and honors Dr. Abdul Kalam has received in recognition of his exceptional contributions in various fields. His accomplishments continue to inspire people around the world and his legacy as a visionary leader, scientist, and statesman remains unparalleled.

Life Lessons and Inspirational Quotes :

Dr. A.P.J. Abdul Kalam was known not only for his remarkable career as a scientist, leader and President of India, but also for his profound wisdom and inspiring words. He often shared valuable life lessons and motivational quotes that continue to inspire people today. Here are some of the life lessons and inspirational quotes of Dr. Abdul Kalam:

Dream, dream, dream: Dr. Kalam believed in the power of dreams and encouraged others to dream big. He said, "Dream, dream, dream. Dreams turn into thoughts, and thoughts lead to action." He stressed the importance of setting ambitious goals and working tirelessly to achieve them.

Failure is the first step to success: Dr. Kalam believed that failure is nothing to be afraid of, but rather a stepping stone to success. He said, "Do not be afraid of failure. Learn from failures and move on." He encouraged people to see failure as an opportunity to learn, grow and improve.

Be a lifelong learner: Dr. Kalam was a strong advocate of continuous learning. He said, "Learning leads to creativity, creativity leads to thinking, thinking leads to knowledge, and knowledge makes you great." He stressed the importance of constantly expanding your skills and knowledge and remaining curious and open-minded throughout your life.

Strive for excellence: Dr. Kalam believed in striving for excellence in everything you do. He said, "Excellence is a continuous process, not an accident." He stressed the importance of consistently striving, being persistent, and never settling for mediocrity.

Believe in yourself: Dr. Kalam encouraged people to believe in their own abilities. He said, "You have to dream before your dreams can come true." He stressed the importance of believing in yourself, having self-confidence, and motivating yourself to succeed.

Be a person of integrity: Dr. Kalam believed in the value of integrity and honesty. He said, "If you want to shine like a sun, you must first burn like a sun." He stressed the importance of being truthful, ethical and responsible in all aspects of life, including personal and professional endeavors.

Serve others selflessly: Dr. Kalam was a true servant leader who believed in the power of service to others. He said, "The best way to find yourself is to lose yourself in service to others." He stressed the importance of giving back to society, helping those in need, and making a positive impact on the lives of others.

Embrace diversity: Dr. Kalam believed in the value of diversity and inclusivity. He said, "Diversity creates dynamism in society." He stressed the importance of embracing diversity in all its forms, including culture, religion, gender, and origin, and promoting an inclusive and harmonious society.

Never give up: Dr. Kalam was a living example of perseverance and resilience. He said, "The difficulties in your life do not come to destroy you, but to help you realize your hidden potential and power." He stressed the importance of never giving up in the face of challenges and instead using them as opportunities for growth and learning.

Leave a legacy: Dr. Kalam believed in leaving a positive legacy. He said, "You have to dream before your dreams can come true." He emphasized the importance of working towards leaving a lasting impact on society and making a meaningful contribution that would inspire future generations.

In conclusion, Dr. A.P.J. Abdul Kalam's life lessons and inspirational quotes continue to inspire millions of people worldwide. His wisdom, vision, and leadership have left an indelible mark on society, and his teachings serve as guiding principles for living a purposeful and meaningful life.

Remembering The Legend :

Dr. A.P.J. Abdul Kalam, fondly referred to as the "President of the People" of India, was an exemplary leader, a scientist and a visionary who left an indelible mark in the hearts and minds of people all over the world. Even after his passing on July 27, 2015, Dr. Kalam's legacy continues to inspire and his memory is cherished by millions. Remembering Dr. A.P.J. Abdul Kalam is not only about honoring his life, but also about internalizing the valuable lessons he imparted and carrying forward his vision for a better world.

Dr. Kalam's life was a true embodiment of hard work, resilience and dedication. Born into a humble family in Rameswaram, a small town in Tamil Nadu, India, he faced numerous challenges and obstacles on his path to success. However, through sheer

determination and perseverance, he
rose to become a renowned scientist
known for his significant contributions
to India's rocket and space programs.
His leadership and vision played a
critical role in the development of
nuclear weapons and ballistic missile
technology in India, earning him the
title "Missile Man of India"

Dr. Kalam's leadership style was
unique and inspirational. He believed
in leading by illustration and had a
strong connect with the youth of India.
He frequently interacted with scholars
and youthful people, encouraging
them to conjure big, work hard, and
contribute to the nation's progress. He
supported for education, invention,
and scientific exploration as crucial
motorists of societal and profitable
development. His speeches, lectures,
and books were filled with wisdom,
provocation, and practical advice,
which continue to inspire people of all

periods to strive for excellence and make a positive impact in their communities. Kalam's modesty, simplicity, and approachability were also remarkable traits that endeared him to people from all walks of life. Despite his multitudinous achievements and accolades, he remained stranded, accessible, and always willing to hear to the voices of the common people. He was known for his warm address, kind words, and gentle smile, which made him a cherished figure not just in India, but across the globe. Kalam's heritage goes beyond his achievements as a scientist and leader. He was a man of deep spiritual beliefs and ethical values. He emphasized the significance of moral and ethical conduct in all aspects of life, and frequently spoke about the need for inclusive development, social justice, and sustainable living. He was a strong advocate for peace, harmony, and interfaith understanding, and worked lifelessly to promote these ideals. Kalam's benefactions and heritage continue to be recognized through colourful enterprises, institutions, and awards named after him. TheA.P.J. Abdul Kalam National Memorial in Rameswaram, India, serves as a homage to his life and achievements, and is visited by thousands of people each time. TheA.P.J. Abdul Kalam Award for Excellence in Teaching and Research, introduced by the Indian government, recognizes outstanding benefactions in the fields of wisdom, technology, and education, in line withDr. Kalam's vision for fostering invention and knowledge creation. In conclusion, flashing back Dr.A.P.J. Abdul Kalam isn't just about commemorating his life and achievements, but also about carrying forward his vision, values, and training.Dr. Kalam's exemplary life, leadership, and wisdom continue to inspire millions of people, and his heritage lives on through the positive impact he made on individualities, communities, and the nation as a whole. As we flash back Dr. Kalam, let us strive to emulate his ideals, work towards a better future, and keep his heritage alive by embodying his training in our studies, words, and conduct.

Printed in Great Britain
by Amazon

42475853R00020